CHRIST AND THE NEW WOMAN

CHRIST AND THE NEW WOMAN

By
CLOVIS G. CHAPPELL

NASHVILLE, TENN.
COKESBURY PRESS

Printed in the United States of America

To

THE FACULTY AND STUDENTS
OF WESLEYAN COLLEGE,
MACON, GA.,
WHO GAVE THESE LECTURES
A MOST GRACIOUS HEARING,
THIS VOLUME IS
RESPECTFULLY DEDICATED
BY THE AUTHOR.

FOREWORD

ON May 22, 1924, Rev. S. R. Belk, D.D., a prominent minister of the North Georgia Conference of the Methodist Episcopal Church South, addressed a communication to the Board of Trustees of Wesleyan College inclosing a check for $2,000 to be used by the Board of Trustees in founding a lectureship.

It was stipulated that the Board of Trustees shall select the lecturer upon the nomination of the Faculty of the College, and the lecturer shall be at liberty to choose his own subject within the realm of practical religion and Christian ethics.

Upon receipt of this communication, the following resolutions were offered and were unanimously adopted:

Resolved: 1. That the Board of Trustees of Wesleyan College has heard with deep gratification the generous offer of Rev. S. R. Belk, D.D., to donate the sum of two thousand dollars ($2,000) for the purpose of founding a lectureship in Wesleyan College.

2. That we gratefully accept the gift and express to Doctor Belk our heartiest appreciation and thank him for his generosity and the splendid spirit which prompts the gift.

3. That the lectureship shall be called "The S. R. Belk Lectureship" in honor of the donor.   W. A. SHELTON,
H. WARNER HILL.

The first of the series was delivered in April of 1927 by Rev. Clovis G. Chappell, D.D., pastor of the First Methodist Church, Memphis, Tenn. These lectures are presented in this volume, and provision is made that the profits arising from the sale of this publication will be added to the lectureship so that when the principal sum shall be sufficiently large an annual series may be provided. The Trustees, Faculty, the student body, and the friends of Wesleyan appreciate deeply this splendid foundation and are pleased that the first series should have been delivered by so representative and distinguished a minister as Dr. Clovis G. Chappell.

W. F. QUILLIAN,
President of Wesleyan College.

Macon, Ga.

CONTENTS

HER OPPORTUNITIES

I

WHEN the historian of a hundred years hence sets himself to the task of interpreting the history of the present century, upon what will he fix his attention as the most important event of this progressive age? What will the world of to-morrow likely regard as the most epoch-making happening that took place in the world of to-day? It will not be our marvelous material prosperity, though to-day has brought to the average laborer luxuries that yesterday were beyond the reach of kings. It will not be any or all the great discoveries in the realm of science. It will not even be the World War, though that was the most costly conflict that any age has yet witnessed. What then will it be? According to Will Durant, the historian of the year A.D. 2000 will look upon the change in the position of woman as the most important and revolutionary event that took place during the twentieth century.

So great has this change been that the modern woman finds herself in a situation that is almost entirely new. This new situation has, of course, in a sense, brought a new woman. That fact it is well for us to face at the beginning. It is not a question of whether you approve of the new woman or disapprove of her. It is not a question of whether you like her or dislike her. She is here. She is a present reality. And what is more, she has come to stay. There was much that was winsome and lovable in the woman of yesterday. But she will never come back. If she ever does, she will come back in the stagecoach and in the prairie schooner. But so long as we face forward, so long will the new woman remain.

It is only truth to say that many of us do object to the new woman. This is not true simply of mere man. There are some men that object, but that is only to be expected. But always the severest critic of woman is woman. We men are rather foolish about you. Furthermore, we flatter ourselves that you have no serious antipathy to us. We men also tend to like each other. But that is where women are in some measure different. They are not quite so quick to like each other. They do not quite so readily believe in each other. Quite often they are exceedingly quick to criticize each other. Therefore, it is fairly

safe to say that there are about as many ob-
jectors to the new woman among her own sex
as there are among the men. But, whether
we object or do not object, the new woman,
I repeat, is here. She is a present fact.

In speaking of the modern woman as new,
however, we do not, of course, mean that she
is different in her essential nature from the
woman of yesterday. Humanity is funda-
mentally the same through the centuries.
Woman is one hemisphere of that humanity.
Therefore, in her fundamental characteristics,
she remains the same yesterday, to-day, and
forever. This, however, is true: the woman
of to-day finds herself possessed of a freedom
that her sister of yesterday did not enjoy.
To-day she is taking her place beside man as
an equal in a way that was undreamed-of
in any age of the past.

To be convinced of this it is necessary only
to realize that from the beginning of history,
and beyond, woman has been regarded as a
subordinate and an inferior. How this came
about it is not our purpose to discuss. But
the fact that she has been regarded as inferior,
even in the most enlightened nations, is one
that cannot be denied. Take Israel, for example. There were many choice women

among the ancient Israelites. Some of these occupied positions of influence and honor. But the constant rule was that woman was regarded as inferior. Whatever honor came to her came through her husband or through her sons. That is, she was honored not for what she was in herself, but for her position as wife and mother. But even as a mother her honor was secondary. When the ancestral line was traced, it was always through the father, never through the mother. Even when Matthew and Luke trace the ancestry of Jesus, they trace it back through Joseph and not through Mary. This is doubly significant, seeing that Joseph was not the father of Jesus at all.

The Greeks were a great and cultured people. But this culture was confined almost entirely to the men. The position of women, especially that of wife and mother, was one of constant subjection and inferiority. The Greek wife was entirely uneducated. The only educated women among the Greeks were the courtesans. These were held in fairly high regard. They mingled with men somewhat on terms of equality. Pericles even married a courtesan, a brilliant woman named Aspasia. But the wife as a rule did not count

as a companion or as an equal. The great
philosopher Aristotle said that the relationship between man and woman was that of
governor and subject. Hesiod's idea of a bad
wife was one that insisted upon eating with
her husband. Among the Romans the wife
had a trifle more freedom and at times more
culture, but here, as elsewhere, she was looked
upon as an inferior.

With the coming of Christianity the position of woman underwent a change. This
new religion spread with great rapidity. Its
growth was especially rapid among two classes,
women and slaves. It is easy to understand
why this was true. It offered to both a new
freedom. It told them that they were of
worth in the scheme of things. How it must
have thrilled them to know that in Christ
Jesus there was neither male nor female,
bond nor free—that is, that every human
soul stood on an equal footing before God,
that neither bondage nor sex was a hindrance
to his recognition and his love! In fact,
Christ taught, as others have pointed out,
that sex is temporal and not eternal. "They
which shall be accounted worthy to obtain
that world . . . neither marry nor are given
in marriage."

But the freedom that woman found in the early Church was soon lost. This was due to the upspringing of a rigid ecclesiasticism that was controlled almost entirely by men. Then came the Dark Ages with their appalling growth of asceticism. The Pope decreed that priests should not marry. The Church began to teach that the marriage relationship was one that was morally inferior to that of celibacy. Many taught that it was positively immoral. Strange to say, the whole blame for the dilemma was laid upon the woman. Man was a child of God, but the woman was a child of the devil. She, therefore, was useful only for the temptation of man. Even the great Augustine said that he thought women might rise from the dead, but if they did they would no longer be capable of tempting men. It never occurred to him, as another has pointed out, that men might be so changed as to cease to be a temptation to women.

During these dark days there were but two respectable positions open to woman. One of them was that of wife, the other was that of nun. She had to become either the bride of some man or the bride of the church. The unmarried woman, as such, did not count. The fact that a woman could not marry made it almost an absolute necessity that she go into a nunnery. If she failed to do either, unless she was highly placed, she was almost absolutely at the mercy of the brutality of that hard age. Therefore, it was woe unto the woman who did not marry. Therefore, also, many married, not because they had a real opportunity, but because they had to.

In Abbotsford, the home of Sir Walter Scott, there is a sketch that tells a story of one of his ancestors. One day this gentleman came to his dinner. When he lifted the cover from the meat dish he found nothing in the dish but his spurs. That meant that his larder was empty. He must go out and hustle for his meat. Now, in the process of sheep-stealing, he was caught by a neighbor and sentenced to be hanged. It so happened, however, that this neighbor had three daughters. The eldest of these was so very far from being beautiful that she seemed doomed to remain single. Her name was Mucklemouth. The mother, knowing that prospective sons-in-law were a bit scarce, did not think that a good man should be foolishly destroyed. Therefore she had her husband propose to set the young man free provided he would marry Mucklemouth. The captive agreed to look her over. This done, he declared that he preferred to be hanged. But she ministered to him so kindly in the days before his execution that he relented, and "they lived happy ever after."

When we come to England and America, we find woman, till very recently, still occupying a thoroughly subordinate position. In fact, to this hour she is rated as inferior by not a few. A writer in one of our leading magazines said only last month that there were but three things in all the world at which man did not excel. One was that of being a mother; the second, the ability to sing soprano; and the third was being able to keep the face smooth without shaving. There is nothing good, this man concludes, that you can say about woman, but that you can answer truthfully, "So's your old man." It is easy to see how this writer regards woman still. And there are many even yet of both sexes that agree with him.

But only a few years ago everybody agreed with him. It has not been long since a husband had the right to collect his wife's wages. It has been only a little longer since he had the right to beat her if he so desired. Some fifty years ago a Boston woman who was

married lost her trunk while traveling by
rail. She sued the railroad in an effort to
recover her loss. But it was of no avail.
She lost her case. Why did she lose? Simply
on the ground that she did not own any
clothes. Her clothes belonged to her husband.
Of course, she still does not have much clothing. But all the flimsy and abbreviated things
she does have are her own. About sixty years
ago the physicians of Philadelphia voted to
excommunicate any doctor who lectured in a
school that allowed women to attend or any
doctor who would consult with a woman
physician. But all this has changed. Our
century has witnessed the dawning of a new
day.

II

What are some of the changes that this
new day has brought?

1. It has brought the woman political
freedom. She has the right to vote. Taxa-
tion without representation has been recognized to be wrong for the woman as well as for
the man. It seems that such a recognition
would have taken place long ago. But the
franchise was only granted to the women in
the United States in the year 1920. This

gives her a voice in the affairs of the nation. She now has a voice in the affairs of her community, and even in the affairs of the school to which her children must go. She has been recognized as being politically equal to her brother.

2. What is far more important than political freedom, she has been granted freedom of choice with regard to her vocation. For many centuries, remember, the range of her choice was circumscribed in the extreme. She could be a wife and mother, or she could be a nun. In comparatively recent years, she was privileged to teach. But even then her opportunities of choice were exceedingly limited. This limiting of choice, of necessity, shut the door in the face of a multitude of capable and worthful women. For, if it is true that men have different tastes and different aptitudes and are suited for different vocations, it is equally true of women. What would appeal to one woman would not necessarily appeal to her sister. I believe it is still true that most women prefer before all others the vocation of wifehood and motherhood. But, while that is true, it is safe to say that it is by no means universally so. Neither are all suited for this high vocation. Neither do all have a

fit opportunity offered for entering upon it. To allow a woman, therefore, to make her own choice and to follow the line of her own aptitude is nothing more than her right. It is also conducive to her highest happiness and to her largest usefulness.

3. Along with this right of choice and of self-expression has come that which goes hand in hand with it, the right of preparation. It is only recently that women have had a fair chance at an education. For instance, in cultured Boston in the early part of the last century, the school board agreed that the girls might have the use of the high school when the boys were not using it. Even as wise a man as John Milton would not allow his daughters to be taught any language other than English, because he thought that one tongue was enough for any woman. I am not saying that up to recently women have not been educated at all. They have for many years been given a certain kind of education. But it was one that was intended to fit the woman into the scheme of man rather than to fit her to live as a separate and independent individual.

To-day this has changed. Our girls have as good opportunity and as free a scope in

the educational world as have our boys.
And they are taking advantage of their opportunities in a marvelous way. There were
twelve times as many girls in high school in
the year 1924 as in 1890, though the population only doubled during that period. There
were five times as many in college. In the
year 1926 there were 224,000 young men in
our colleges and universities and 152,000
young women. And these were giving quite
as good account of themselves as were their
brothers.

4. The new day has also brought to woman
a new independence by virtue of her better
and more practical education. She has a
capacity for taking care of herself that did not
belong to the woman of yesterday. There
was a time when many women had to marry
in order to have a home. She was incapable
of taking care of herself. If she was left with
an estate, she had to marry to save herself
from the stigma of being an old maid. There
was nothing that was so much dreaded by the
woman of a few years ago as being condemned
to remain unmarried. It was a species of
disgrace. Such were called, cynically, "the
army of the unenjoyed." Every crude and

cruel joke that man's ingenuity could invent was told at their expense.

But this painful dependence has now passed. In fact, the old maid no longer exists. She belongs to our dead and buried past. Years ago you could spot her in any crowd. She wore a dress that at once touched her ears and swept the ground. I am told that she wore yarn hose, though that is pure hearsay, as no one ever saw her ankles. Her occupation was knitting, crocheting, and looking after the children of her fortunate married sister. But all this has changed. "She has cast away her flannels," her high shoes, her long skirt, her woolen stockings, and her long hair. She has dropped her knitting and nurse-playing and gone to work out in the big world. She can now remain single and not be sneered at. No woman has to marry to-day unless she gets a chance. She once felt compelled to marry without much of a chance. But the woman of to-day enjoys a new independence.

There is another aspect to this independence. As the new woman does not have to marry unless she wishes, neither does she have to remain married if that relationship appears unbearable and intolerable. There was a time when the divorced woman was in utter disre-

pute. She was under a terrible cloud. For
this reason many a woman has gone on living
with her husband when her married life was
a distasteful and repellent thing. This she
did because she did not feel that she could
face the bitter hell of the disgrace that was
sure to be the result of a divorce. Then there
was an added reason for her suffering in silence.
If she left her husband, there was no way that
she could make a living But if the modern
woman finds her married life impossible, she
can go her own way without fear of either
disgrace or poverty.

5. Then this new day has brought to woman
deliverance from the bondage of a double
standard of morals. There has not been a
nation in all history where virtue was not
expected and required of the wife. But until
the coming of Christianity there was not a
nation where virtue was either required or
expected of the man. Even in spite of Christianity, we have gone on for centuries demanding that our women be lily-white while
we ourselves had the privilege of walking the
path of pitch. But that also belongs to the
past. To-day what is wrong for the woman is
wrong for the man, and what is right for the
man is right for the woman. Whether the

morals of both will be raised by this change or lowered by it remains to be seen. But this is certainly true: both are henceforth going to be judged by the same standard.

6. This new day, by bringing woman a larger culture and a larger field of activity, has also brought opportunity for an increase of strength. She is having to struggle with temptations that are new to her. She is having to carry a heavier load. This should prove helpful rather than hurtful. It is not by the dangers dodged, but by difficulties met and overcome, that we become strong. That is but a poor kind of righteousness that is born of a lack of opportunity to go wrong. "I cannot praise a fugitive, cloistered virtue, unexercised and unbreathed, that never sallies forth to meet its adversary where garlands are to be run for not without heat and dust."

Whether the woman of to-day and to-morrow will in reality be better than the woman of yesterday remains to be seen. That she is going to be stronger there is no doubt. In fact, she is already so. She is far more efficient and far more capable of taking care of herself. She already strides with confidence among difficulties that leave some of her elders bewildered. Many a modern

mother is at her wit's end. She is filled with
deadly fear for her wild and venturesome
daughter. But the girl is not at all afraid.
To see the two together is to be reminded of
nothing so much as of a sweet old hen cluck-
ing anxiously on the shores of a pond while
her growing child, that chances to be a duck-
ling, is disporting itself in the water with
great relish and without fear.

III

These are some of the changes that our day
has brought. They are changes, in the main,
I am convinced, that have taken place according to the will of God. I do not believe
for a moment that he ever purposed that
woman should be a subjected and subordinate
creature. Sex in itself cannot rightly be a
badge of inferiority. We are never to be alike,
but we can be equal. We can come to our
best in no other way. The roadway to the
highest is indicated by these words, "Two
heads in council, two beside the hearth, two
in the tangled business of the world."

Now, the question that I bring to you young
women is this: What are you going to do with
the fine opportunities that in the providence
of God have come to you? You have a big

chance that was far beyond the reach of your
mothers. What are you to do about it?
Broadly speaking, two courses are open to
you.

1. You may use this large freedom selfishly.
Having declared your independence of many
of the time-worn customs that shackled your
mothers, you may even go further and declare
your independence of those fundamental integrities by which the soul lives and by which
civilization is held together. You may fancy
that you can even fling over the moral law.
You may take the road of crass selfishness.
You may even get so drunk upon your new
freedom that you will become convinced that
you can live your own life without serious
regard to your obligations to either God or
man. But, if you take this course, I warn
you that your new opportunities will prove
an utter curse both to yourselves and to the
world.

2. But there is another and higher road open
to you. You may take the way of the un-
selfish heart. You may realize that every
new capacity, every new opportunity brings
with it a new obligation. About the finest
thing that even Jesus ever said was this,
"For their sakes I sanctify myself, that they

also may be sanctified." In his name I dare to call you to this high self-consecration. If you refuse, you will help our civilization to rot down. But if you accept the challenge of this new day, you can have a large part in the remaking of our shattered and broken world. The key to the door that leads unto that Christ-conquered day of our dreams where there shall be a reign of righteousness is more largely in your hands than ever before. Surely you have come to the kingdom for such a time as this.

AS A WORKER OUTSIDE THE HOME

I

In speaking of woman as a worker, we are in no sense putting her into a new rôle. It is not at all novel or startling that so many women of our day are working. Women have always worked. "Let the Women Do the Work" may pass for a new song among those who have forgotten their history. It may be sung jestingly by the thoughtless. But those who are wiser know that this song is by no means a product of our progressive age. It is older than literature. It is older than civilization. It was a favorite male chorus, sung not jestingly, but in sober earnestness, countless centuries before the building of the pyramids.

But there is something new about the present situation, and that is that the modern woman is now engaged at tasks that the woman of yesterday would never have dreamed of undertaking. Her range of vocational choice is practically as wide as that of man, and she is zestfully trying her hand at all kinds of work. She is entering business, industry, professional life. In fact, wherever work is being done she seems bent upon presenting herself. The census of 1920 showed that there were then five hundred and seventy-two different classes of work being done in the United States. It showed further that women were engaged in five hundred and thirty-seven of those occupations. That is, there were then only thirty-five different classes of work that were for men only. This number has in all probability been reduced since then. Thus it is evident that the modern woman is courageously trying to enter into her possession.

Not only are women going into many varied vocations, but they are going in great numbers. Our present century has witnessed an exodus from the home that is absolutely unparalleled and, to some, appalling. The woman who goes out day by day to some particular task is no longer an exception. On the contrary, she seems on the way to be becoming the rule. It is estimated that there are now between eight and ten millions of women in the United States who are employed outside the home. This means that one-fifth, or possibly as many as one-fourth, of all the women in this country are now engaged in outside work. In England, the percentage is far greater. One authority states that fifty per cent of all the women in England are now gainfully employed outside the home.

II

How has this change in woman's sphere of work come about? I think it safe to say that it has not taken place because of any deliberate plan or purpose on the part of either men or women. The suffragettes of the aggressive and militant type may feel that they had much to do with this consummation, but in my opinion they have had very little to do with it. The Nineteenth Amendment to the Constitution is not responsible for this development. There is no group nor combination of groups that can take the unction to themselves that they have by deliberate purpose brought about this stupendous change.

It is equally safe to say that this revolution is not the result of any fundamental change that has taken place in woman herself. Women are naturally conservative. They are more so than men. By nature, they are lovers of home. Some six or seven years ago a questionnaire was sent to a number of young women who were college graduates. Among the questions asked was this: Were it necessary for you to give up your career or the prospect of marriage and home-making, which would you surrender? There were five hundred and ninety-five responses to this question. Twenty-two were undecided. Fifty-one declared that they would give up the prospects of marriage. Five hundred and twenty-two said that they would surrender their careers in favor of wifehood and motherhood. I doubt whether the home would to-day receive so large a majority. However, this is an indication that the change in woman's sphere of work has not come as a result of any great change in woman herself.

Whence then has it come? It is the result of the changes, economic and industrial, that have taken place in our modern world. It is a situation that is the outcome of changed conditions rather than of changed personalities. For instance, there are many tasks that were once performed in the home, or in connection with the home, that are now performed in the outside world. To so great an extent is this the case that there is no longer sufficient work in connection with the keeping of the home to guarantee a job to every woman. The world has never before been faced by such a condition. In other days, the average woman not only had enough work to do, but often far more than enough. The primitive woman, for instance, was by no means a lady of leisure. She did the work that was most prosaic and monotonous. She cleared and tilled the soil. She prepared the food. She was the drudge. The man did the more exciting and romantic tasks, the hunting, the fishing, and the fighting.

During the pioneer days the weight of home duties was still very heavy upon the shoulders of the woman. At that time the home was far more than a dwelling place. It was a factory where many different industries were carried on. The woman, as a rule, had to be the organizer and general manager of this institution. By the time she did, or had others to do, the spinning of the thread, the weaving of this thread into cloth, and the making of this cloth into garments, together with the countless other duties necessary to the administration of her household, she had given a good account of herself. In fact, her contribution to the upkeep of the family was often quite as large as, if not even larger than, that of her husband.

Even so recently as my own boyhood, the home was far less dependent upon the outside

world than it is to-day. This was especially
true of those living on farms. It was often
little less true of those living in villages and
towns. There were, therefore, then many
tasks that were regarded as woman's work
that have since been taken out of the home
either in part or in whole. For instance, when
I was a boy on the farm, we obtained our milk
and butter by first-hand acquaintance with
the cow. To this end, we had to have milk-
maids. I was one myself. The milk thus
secured had to be strained, carried to the
spring house, skimmed, and churned. Some
of the most dreary and humiliating moments
of my life were spent with one of my mother's
aprons tied, not around my waist, but around
my neck, to protect my clothes while I en-
joyed the thrill of operating a churn-dasher.
But to-day even those on farms are relieved
of much of the drudgery of this work. For
us in towns and cities it is removed altogether.
Our milk is put upon our doorstep each morning, and our butter is brought by the grocery-
man.

In former days our beds and bedclothes
were made mainly at home. When we wanted
new beds and pillows, we picked the geese.
When new quilts were wanted, they had to be

made. And what a task it was! The top part of the quilt was made of countless little pieces of cloth that had to be patiently sewed together. And, what is stranger still, cloth was often cut to pieces just to give some already overtaxed woman the privilege of sewing it back. When this work of art was completed, it was spread over a lining with cotton batting in between, suspended on quilting frames, and quilted. The finished product was quite serviceable and often more colorful than Joseph's coat. But to-day we find it far cheaper to buy such necessities ready-made.

So it is with endless other articles. We used to make much of our soap. We gathered our fruit and canned it. Our sewing was done largely at home. Our laundry was done there. Our cooking was done there. Our eating was done there. In fact, when a baby came it was born at home. When a member of the family was sick, that member was sick at home. When loved ones died, they died at home. When they were buried, they were buried from home.

To-day this has in large measure changed. We buy our soap ready-made. The factory can make it cheaper and better. We find that by the time we buy the fruit and the sugar

and go to the trouble of canning we can buy
the finished product cheaper than we can
produce it.   We buy most of our clothing
ready-made.   We send our soiled linen to the
laundry.   We buy much of our bread from
the baker.   We do a good bit of our eating at
the restaurant or hotel.   We are born at the
hospital.   We are taken there when we are
sick.   When the end comes we die there.
Then, often enough, we are buried from some
funeral home.   Most of us still sleep at home,
but that is about all that can be counted on
with absolute certainty.

But the fact that many tasks once performed in the home are now performed there
no longer does not mean that these have been
discontinued altogether.   They are being
carried on elsewhere on a larger scale than
ever before.   In addition, there are endless
forms of work being done to-day that yesterday were almost or altogether unknown.
For instance, in 1870 there were only one
hundred and fifty-four stenographers and
typists in all the United States.   This included
both men and women.   To-day you can find
that number in a single average office building.
Then there are enormous industries now that
did not exist a few years ago.   Take the auto-

mobile industry for example.   Thus, while
opportunities for work within the home have
been constantly decreasing, opportunities outside the home have been increasing far more
rapidly.

In the light of these facts, it is easy to understand woman's exodus from the home.   The
need for her there has greatly diminished.
The need without the home has greatly increased.   The old cry of "Back to the kitchen"
is in many instances a vain and futile cry.
There is no longer room in the kitchen.   If all
women were to return to the kitchen, there
would not even be standing room.   Besides,
there are many that have no kitchen to which
to return, nor will they ever have.   If the
women of to-day are to work at all, many of
them must work outside the home.   To refuse
to do so would be to remain in utter idleness.

III

Those gainfully employed outside the home
may be divided roughly into three classes.

1. There are those who must work in order
to make a living.   Multitudes of women engaged in industrial, business, and professional
work to-day are so employed for the very
same reason that men are.   They are working

in order to support themselves and those who may be dependent upon them. Many are girls from homes where the salary of the father is inadequate. Often these must not only support themselves, but help to bear the burden of the family. Not a few are widows who have been left without income. Some of these have children that must be fed and clothed. Work outside the home, therefore, is for many women a necessity. This is true of the majority of those thus employed.

2. Next are those who are under no economic pressure. They have comfortable homes, and their financial needs are adequately supplied. But, while they do not have to work in order to make a living, they are convinced that they must work in order to make a life. They could get on fairly well without a salary, but would be miserable without a job. These do not feel that the accident of inherited wealth should condemn them to the wretchedness of playing the parasite. This class is composed mainly of young, unmarried women whose parents are in easy circumstances.

Now, the fact that these prefer to work outside the home rather than remain idle within the home is altogether commendable. Idleness is a road that always leads down hill.

It is a short cut to restlessness and unhappi-
ness.   Idlers, both male and female, are a
menace to themselves and to others.   Huxley
was right in saying that a sense of uselessness
is the greatest shock that can come to a living
organism.   No one can be satisfied by a life
of pampered idleness.   For life to be worth
the living there must be a worthy and taxing
purpose for which to live.   It is better to work
in a pigsty than to do nothing in a flower
garden.

The world has not always believed this.
Once there were those who taught that work
was a curse.   I heard this heresy when I was
a boy, though from what source I do not now
remember.   But I do remember that I readily
accepted the statement.   But with the passing
of the years I have reached a conclusion that
is entirely opposite.   Work is a blessing.   It
is a help in resisting temptation.   How often
we do the wrong simply because we are not
engaged in some worthful task!   It is a means
of grace.   It is a roadway to usefulness.   It is
often one of the best comforts to a broken
heart.   Certainly Kingsley was right when he
said that we ought to thank God every morning that we have something to do that day,
whether we want to do it or not.   And to this,

I am sure, many young women who have turned from possible idleness to earnest toil heartily agree.

3. Finally, there are those who have turned from the home from choice. Some of these go because the particular task at which they desire to work is in the outside world. They have fixed their hearts on some definite career, and the realization of their ambition is put before all else. Possibly, if a suitable opportunity offers, they will marry. They may perchance become mothers. But even the high privilege of wifehood and motherhood is regarded by them as secondary. It will be renounced altogether if it clashes with the one purpose on which the heart is set.

Then there are some who elect to leave the home, not to realize some definite ambition, but merely to escape the duties and responsibilities of the home. These have taken too seriously present-day tirades against the slavery of the home. They fail to recognize that the so-called slavery of many of their sisters is a far finer something than their freedom. Those leaving the home from choice, whether to attain or to escape, are in my opinion the smallest of the three classes mentioned. Some are fine and heroic. Some are merely mistaken. The majority are likely to realize at the last that they have been cheated, that at best they have attained only the secondary.

IV

The woman who works outside the home still has a few handicaps to overcome. There are factors without and within that militate against her success. Let me mention some of these.

1. Prejudice. There are still those who resent the fact that women are now privileged to work as freely as men. These are perfectly willing that she should do certain kinds of work, but maintain that there are others in which she has no place. For instance, man does not like her in a managerial position. It is an affront to his dignity to take orders from her. You see, man is still somewhat in possession of his superiority complex. He believes he can beat woman doing almost anything. He often believes he ought to be paid more for doing the same thing. And not infrequently he is. To get a position over a male competitor, it is usually necessary for the woman to be able to do the job not a little better, but far better. To get as good salary she must do, not as much, but more.

2. A second handicap is the fact that woman sometimes expects consideration because of her sex. Of course this is, in a measure, quite natural. When men meet her they tip their hats. On the street cars they give her a seat—sometimes. To cherish such expectation, however, is a mistake. The woman who does so will find herself greatly hampered. She will be too personal in her attitude toward her employer. When he tells her that her poor typing will not go, or that she ought to be on time, or that it would be better for her to carry on her courtship over her own telephone, after office hours, she is apt to take it as a personal insult and to burst into tears and say that she is too sensitive to be talked to after that fashion. Happy is the woman who recognizes the fact that in order to succeed she must depend upon her efficiency and upon that alone.

3. A third handicap is a lack of a worthy ambition. This is quite often a fault of young men as well as of young women. A few weeks ago a young fellow dropped out of the Medical Department of our university in order to take up some petty job that had no promise of any worthy goal. The trouble with that young man is that he is satisfied to live for to-day.

He is getting enough to eat and enough to wear; therefore he takes no thought for the morrow. The same is true of a great many working girls. All they ask is enough to make them independent. Their goal is attained when they are able to buy the clothing on which they have set their hearts. Oftentimes they are even satisfied when they have demonstrated to their friends that they are capable of making their own way. Such a cheap ambition cannot bring a woman to her best possibilities. In order to do our best work, we must aim at a worth-while goal.

4. Then the woman worker is often hampered by the lack of a far view. The young man entering upon a professional or business career usually does so with the expectation of continuing throughout life. With the girl this is often different. She does not regard her position as a life-long proposition. Her job is often little more than a waiting station where she stops over for the Matrimonial Express. Of course she is not to be blamed in the least for getting on that train if it comes by. But the trouble is, it might never come. Therefore I cannot but advise that she make her temporary quarters as agreeable as pos-

sible. Her stay in them may be indefinitely prolonged.

5. The final handicap that I mention is divided interests. Not a few of those engaged in business to-day are mothers. Now, the working mother has two tasks on her hands, either of which is big enough to enlist about all her energies. This is certainly true of the task of child-rearing. For this reason it is my firm conviction that no mother ought to do full-time work outside the home unless she has to. There are mothers, I know, who like such work. The call of the outside world is strong upon them. But I venture to say that it is no stronger than the call of the heart of the children for the mother. This is true regardless of how good and capable may be the help that she hires to look after her children. There is absolutely nobody that can take the place of the mother.

I read an article recently by a woman who before her marriage was an editorial writer of rare ability. She is now a wife and mother. Recently she has been offered a place on the editorial staff of a leading paper at a salary far larger than she received before her marriage. But she refused it because she believed that her children were of more value to her

than her career. When her boy rushes in
from school, the first word he shouts when
entering the door is "mother." "I hurry,"
she says, "to find what he wants. He speaks
as if he had some most important matter on
hand. But his answer to my inquiry is, 'I
just wanted to know if you were there.'"
And this mother is convinced that there is
nothing so important for the mother as being
there. Of course, there are some mothers that
must work. It is the only way to keep the
children from want. But such women are
hampered. They are undertaking the work
of two. Some are carrying on both tasks with
admirable heroism. But, as a rule, the task
of being a mother is big enough.

V

But, regardless of all handicaps, woman is
entering industrial, business, and professional
life and succeeding. This she is doing in spite
of the fact that many of us felt about her
doing this work a bit as Doctor Johnson did
about her preaching, "Sir, a woman's preaching is like a dog's standing on his hind legs;
it is not well done, but the wonder is that it
should be done at all." But woman is doing
her work and doing it well. Moreover, I think

it safe to say that she has not lowered the moral tone of any sphere into which she has entered. On the contrary, she has had the opposite effect. Whatever she has touched she has touched to make cleaner. Therefore it is safe to conclude that woman is working helpfully outside the home and will continue to do so.

It is my opinion, however, that the woman of to-morrow will narrow her range of vocation rather than widen it. To-day she is experimenting. She is demonstrating. She is testing her powers. She is proving to herself and to the world that she can do a man's work. Having proved her case, she will turn more and more to those tasks for which she has a natural fitness. In fact, I am optimist enough to believe she will be even less eager to escape from the home than is the woman of to-day. She will see more clearly than now that success in a career, while fine and worthful, falls just short of the highest. Not outside the home, but within it, will the woman of to-morrow, as of yesterday, find her fullest life and make her largest contribution.

IN THE HOME

I

IT is a truism to say that in considering the home we are considering the institution of supreme importance. Whatever is wrong in the individual, whatever is wrong in the nation can almost always be traced to the home. The home is the fountain from which issue the streams that make the great river of our national life. If the fountain is impure, the stream is of necessity impure. If the home is unchristian, our individual and national life will also be unchristian. If we are moral and spiritual failures in the home, we are going to be moral and spiritual failures everywhere.

It is equally true that whatever is of worth in the life of the individual or in the life of the nation can be traced to the home. If we have respect and reverence for those integrities that hold our civilization together, it is because we learned that respect in the home. If we are law-abiding, if we have due respect for constituted authority, it is, as a rule, because we learned those lessons in the home. If we are Christian in our thinking, and Chris-

tian in our living, the chances are over-
whelmingly great that we were born and
trained in Christian homes. In short, we are
just as good or just as bad as our home life
makes us.

It is easy to understand why this is true.
The home receives us in the very earliest
morningtide of life. It has the shaping of our
characters during those days when they are
most impressionable. It is next to impossible
to change a giant of the forest. If it has become gnarled and knotted, it is quite certain
that it will remain so to the end. But if it is
taken in hand when it is only a tender twig,
then it can be made into something of grace
and beauty. The impressions of our early
home life are the ones that abide. It is exceedingly hard to recover in later life if the
influences of our young and tender years have
made for evil. Equally true is it that it is
hard finally to break away from the gripping
influences and the clinging memories of a
genuinely Christian home.

If you were reared in such a home, its spell
is upon you to this hour. You doubtless
count the memory of it as one of the choicest
possessions that life has brought you. How

many of us who are getting on into the years
can sing with real fervor and appreciation,

"How dear to my heart are the scenes of my childhood,
  When fond recollection presents them to view;
The orchard, the meadow, the deep-tangled wildwood,
  And every loved spot which my infancy knew!"

As I sing it I can see once more the home of
my boyhood. There is the old white house
under the hill with the sturdy apple trees in
front of it and the forest of beech, oak, and
chestnut stretching away in the distance back
of it. There is the old farm, fenced in by the
silver thread of the Buffalo River. I can hear
the lowing of the cattle, the neighing of the
horses, the merry tinkling of bells. Above all
else, I can see the loved faces that made home
what it was. There was a father there who
knew how to pray and a mother whose face
was sweet with the peace of a great discovery.
The atmosphere was distinctly Christian.
Therefore it is not to be wondered at that its
sanctifying influence is upon my heart to this
hour.

II

What is the influence of the new woman
upon the home? We are hoping that in the
end she is going to be a better and wiser home

builder than was her sister of the past. But I am convinced that this is at present a hope rather than a realized fact. Just now the woman seems to me to be more of a peril to the home than otherwise. In stating fully my reason for this conviction, it will be necessary for me to include a few facts to which I have called attention in a previous lecture. The new woman is a present peril to the home for the following reasons:

1. She is less likely to establish a home.

(1) She marries less readily than did her mother or grandmother. I do not mean by this that the mating instinct is less strong within her. I do not mean that she is in any sense averse to the marriage relation should her demands be fully met. But to-day she is in a far better position to make demands than ever before. Marriage is no longer so close akin to an absolute necessity. Nor is it always under the existing circumstances the most desirable thing to do. This is true for many reasons. Among them let me mention the following:

(a) The economic pressure has been removed. The new woman is able to take care of herself. In other days it was often necessary for a woman to marry in order to be sure of a living. A husband was almost an absolute necessity because she had to be taken care of, and because he was the most logical one to perform that important task. But this has changed. The new woman does not need anyone to take care of her. She is at home in the business and professional world. She is so amply able to take care of herself that all economic pressure has for very many been removed.

(b) Then she is often in love with her work. This is true whether she is in business or professional life. She finds that she has a natural gift and a natural love for it. She likes its contacts. She likes its freedom. She feels that the work is far more to her taste than would be the task of keeping a home. She would much prefer to go to business every morning at nine o'clock and quit at four or five than to start earlier with her home duties and never quit at all. She would rather give herself to her nursing, or to her buying and selling, or to her clerical work than to give herself to the sweeping of the same floors and the dusting of the same furniture and the planning and wondering what she is going to prepare for breakfast, lunch, and dinner to-day and to-morrow and on and on to the end of the chapter.

(*c*) Not only does the new woman often like her job, but she especially likes the remuneration that comes with it. She has grown accustomed to having money of her own to spend as she pleases. If she wants a new dress or a new hat, she can buy it without having to go through the sometimes trying and embarrassing ordeal of wheedling the price out of a grudging and close-fisted husband. In short, this new woman has become a bit of a capitalist. It is often a very new rôle for her, but it is very much to her liking. Therefore it is not at all surprising that she tends to respond less quickly to an offer of marriage than did the woman of yesterday.

(2) Not only is it true that the modern woman is less eager for marriage than the woman of yesterday, but it is equally true that she is less eagerly sought. Her waning enthusiasm for entering into the marriage relationship is no more pronounced than the waning enthusiasm on the part of the modern man in seeking her for this sacred partnership. Since this is the case, it is not surprising that there is to-day a falling off in the number of marriages in proportion to the population.

This is a bad sign. If such tendency is not checked, it bodes great ill for the future. In fact, I know of no surer road to utter disaster than an ever-increasing aversion on the part of both women and men to assume the high privileges and responsibilities of marriage. Such a course could have no goal but moral and racial bankruptcy.

But whence comes this cooling zeal for marriage on the part of men? Are we to conclude that we are now confronted by a new man as well as by a new woman? No, that is not the case. I am convinced that it is the changed attitude of woman that has brought about this changed attitude on the part of man. We have given some reasons for the prevailing decline of zeal for marriage on the part of woman. But why, I repeat, is there a corresponding decline on the part of man? It arises, I think, chiefly from the fact that the modern woman as a rule demands more of her prospective husband than did the woman of the past.

(a) First, she demands more financially. Away back in the primitive days when I was married, it was not necessary for the groom to possess a fortune. He did not even have to have a large salary. Had such been the case,

I have an idea that my wife would have missed the best chance she ever had. But in those days young people were willing to face poverty together. So often to-day this is not the case. Here is a girl, for instance, who is making a salary of a hundred to a hundred and fifty dollars per month. She is going with a young man who wants to marry her. But his salary is no larger than her own. Hence he often has not the rashness to ask her to marry him. The fact that he knows that he cannot give her as much as she is accustomed to have humiliates him and drives him off. Even if he is bold enough to press his suit by bringing to bear the antiquated argument that two can live as cheaply as one, she is likely to be too wise to believe it. Hence marriage is postponed till he can make a larger income. Oftentimes the result of this postponement is that, by the time they are ready to marry, they have lost all desire to marry. This type of demand may be right at times, but as a rule it is absolutely wrong. It helps to account for the fact that there are by estimate six millions of men in the United States to-day between twenty-one and thirty who are not married.

(b) Then the new woman demands more intellectually. This is, of course, as it should be. She is better educated than the woman of yesterday. Being better educated, she naturally demands more education on the part of her husband. But here is one radical difference between man and woman. It is a difference that is as abiding as the law of gravitation. A man can be fairly happy with a woman that he knows to be inferior to himself both in education and intelligence. But a woman cannot be happy with a man who is her inferior. The man insists upon being looked up to. He simply cannot be happy without it. The woman just as earnestly insists upon looking up to the man she loves. The highest happiness is impossible for her without it. Mark you, I am not undertaking to say why this is the case. But that it is the case I believe few thoughtful observers will deny.

Now, since this is true, you can readily see that the highly-educated woman is at a disadvantage so far as getting married is concerned. Her chances of a desirable marriage decrease in proportion to the increase of her culture. A young college woman recently complained bitterly that a girl had to be a bit of a moron in order to appeal to men. Of course, that is putting it too strongly. But this much is true: our sex just has to feel its superiority. Of course this becomes next to impossible for the half-educated man in the presence of a thoroughly educated woman. In the presence of such a woman, such a man feels uncomfortable. And if a woman makes a man feel uncomfortable, take it from me, she will never get him.

Now, my girl, if you really want that "dumb-bell" who is going with you, I can tell you how to get him. Make him think that he is saying something when he is not. Put a sparkle of interest in your eye at his insipid attempts at carrying on a conversation. Laugh gleefully at his inane and threadbare jokes. Send him away with a conviction that he has been highly entertaining. Compel him to think well of himself. In so doing, as surely as two and two make four, you will lead him to think well of you. By nature, I repeat, we are eager to be looked up to. If, therefore, you are too high to look at us in any other way except with the downward look, you have lost your opportunity with us.

(c) In some instances the new woman in making her choice of a husband is demanding more morally. This is as it should be. Some few are doing so for religious reasons. They

are themselves vitally Christian. But even
where there is no religious reason for making
such demand it is sometimes done as a measure
of safety. Even those who think lightly of
Christianity have had to face the fact that
what a man sows, that he also reaps. He reaps
it in his own poisoned mind and his own
poisoned body. Sad to say, he often reaps it
in the blighted lives of those closest to him,
his wife and his children. Hence some women
are making moral demands. The tragedy is
that the number doing so is not greater.

2. The new woman, in the second place,
tends to be a peril to her home because she
is quicker to wreck it than ever before. An
investigation conducted by Miss Beatrice
Hinkle discloses the fact that divorces have
increased seventy-five per cent during the last
ten years. She further points out that this appalling increase is not due to the revolt of men,
but to the revolt of women. For every one
man who sues for a divorce there are four
women. That is, eighty per cent of all our
divorces are being obtained by women. Thus
it is evident that the new woman has not so
far made for the stabilizing of the marriage
relationship and the strengthening of the

home.   She has decidedly made for the opposite.

Why is this true?

(1) Here again we meet the influence of her
economic independence.   When a woman
had to continue with her husband or be sup-
ported by charity, she was naturally very
slow to seek a divorce.   Under such circumstances, she endured much neglect and in-
justice and even positive cruelty.   This she
did countless multitudes of times.   Over and
over again she kept up a relationship that was
altogether revolting.   She went on living with
a man when she knew that he was nothing
more than a moral leper.   This she felt she
must do because there was no way of making
a living in case of separation.   But that compelling reason has now largely passed.

(2) She is less shackled by public opinion.
In other days women often continued in the
marriage relation when it was disgusting to
her, because she was afraid of blasting her
reputation.   To be divorced was to be dis-
graced.   Even in my boyhood when a grass
widow came into the community people
whispered about her.   They lifted their hands
in horror.   She was a creature to be avoided.
She had lost her crown.   Therefore, it is not

surprising that a woman would often endure the most extreme torture to save herself and, if there were children, to save them from the stigma of shame that was sure to result from her obtaining a divorce.

(3) Then children were once a compelling reason for keeping the home together. But such is not to so great an extent the case now. Too often there are no children. Many married couples regard children as a nuisance. Therefore they avoid this needless responsibility. Of course divorce is easier if the marriage is childless. I think it is safe to say that many a marriage that has gone upon the rocks might have been saved if there had been a child to lay hold on the hand of mother and the hand of father and bind the two together.

3. Then the new woman is often a peril to the home, even when it remains intact. This is true:

(1) Because many wives are now engaged in work outside the home. These, if they begin work in the early days of married life, too seldom become mothers. This in itself makes it impossible for them ever to be home-makers in the truest and best sense. Then there are wives who are also mothers that work outside the home. Some do so from

choice, while others do so because they must. They are under pressure of economic necessity. But, whether from choice or from necessity, such a course is usually a calamity. No home can reach its best when the mother is never present except after working hours.

(2) But what is even more serious is the growing number of wives and mothers who have largely forsaken the home, not in order to work, but in order to play. We complain much to-day of the swiftness of youth. But theirs is a mere snail's pace in comparison with that of many of our youngish married women. Half-drunk with their new sense of freedom, some have refused to become mothers at all. Others have brought children into the world only to neglect them. They have flung their responsibilities on to other shoulders. They have resigned in favor of the nurse, the kindergarten, the day school, the streets, and the movies. They are so rushed in the pursuit of pleasure that they haven't time for the building of a real home and the mothering of their own children.

Now, I am not so foolish as to believe that a wife and mother should spend all her time at home. But certainly it is equally true that she should not spend all her time away from it. Real motherhood is always costly. We might as well face that fact. "There stood by the cross of Jesus his mother." That is the mother's position through the years. It has aways been so. It will be so forever. But if the mother has acquaintance above others with the cross, she is also crowned above all others. If she pays the greatest price, she also reaps the richest reward. "She looketh well to the ways of her household"; therefore "her children rise up and call her blessed."

III

But if the hands of the new woman are full of peril, they are also full of possibilities. She surely has it within her power to be the finest wife and mother and the best home builder that we have yet known. It is my dream that this is going to be the final outcome. I dare to cherish this hope for the following reasons:

1. Some of the causes that make the new woman a present peril will ultimately make her a greater asset in real home-making. The fact, for instance, that she is better educated than formerly is not going permanently to frighten the man away. It is going to serve to make him measure up. There will be more

marriages upon a basis of the right kind of equality. Those thus marrying will be in a truer sense mated. In addition, the new woman will bring to her task of housekeeping and child-training a knowledge of scientific method and of child psychology that will make her the most capable mother that the world has yet seen.

Then the fact that woman is now in position to demand more of man morally ought certainly to prove of immeasurable worth. This will surely be the case if woman refuses to strike her flag to the god of the coarse and the unclean. If she only has the courage and the conscience to demand of man what he has always demanded of her, then the home is going to become a purer and happier place, and civilization is going to move into a new day.

2. Finally, there are other of these perils that are, in my opinion, only passing and temporary. They belong, let us hope, to the period of transition through which woman is now passing. I do not believe, for instance, that the present growing indifference to marriage is going to abide. The mating and homing instinct is too deeply implanted. After this new woman has tested her powers, after

she has claimed her freedom, after she has demonstrated her ability to do a man's work, then she will turn with a new zest to that highest of vocations which is peculiarly and exclusively her own: that of mothering the race. Here the woman of to-morrow, as the woman of yesterday, will find at once her highest usefulness and her highest blessedness.

HER DANGERS

I

OUR day is often spoken of as the golden age of woman. It is only natural that it should be so. The modern woman is now in possession of a fullness of freedom such as has belonged to no other generation of women in all history. Freedom is, of course, a great boon and blessing. Ten thousand eulogies have been uttered in its praise. A thousand battle fields have run red with blood in an effort to achieve it. Countless lives have been sacrificed joyfully in its defense. Therefore it is not necessary to argue that freedom, real freedom, is a great benediction.

But, while freedom is a blessing, it is not always an unmixed blessing. In fact, whether it helps or hinders depends upon whether or not those to whom it is granted are ready for it. If history proves anything with emphasis, it is that freedom, coming suddenly to those who are inadequately prepared, brings with it, at least at the first, grave dangers. The French Revolution is a striking example. The people suddenly became free. In so doing

they became a menace. They robbed France
of her best blood and brains, and the nation
has not fully recovered from its tragic losses
to this day.

Now, while I am as far as possible from
classing the modern woman with the French
peasant of that distant day, yet I cannot close
my eyes to the fact that her sudden freedom
is not altogether without its dangers. Some
of these dangers are, in my opinion, passing
and temporary. They belong to the period
of transition and readjustment. But, whatever their nature, they should be faced and
fought, both for the good of women themselves
and for the good of society as a whole. Whatever threatens woman threatens all else that
is of worth. Therefore the only reasonable
course is to look our foes in the face and to
prepare ourselves to meet them bravely and
victoriously.

II

What are some of the dangers that confront
the modern woman?

1. The modern woman is in danger of push-
ing her freedom too far. Freedom does not
mean the privilege of doing absolutely as we
please. Nobody is, or can be, thus free. As

long as we are in any organized society, we are put under certain restraints. To be free of them, one would have to be a second Robinson Crusoe. But even he was not absolutely free. He was hemmed in by the sea. He was constrained by the laws of hunger and thirst. He was compelled to the task of sleeping and waking. No man, anywhere, is ever entirely free. Yet the modern girl often says with a toss of her head, "I am going to live my own life." By that she means, "I am going to do as I please under all circumstances and at all costs." But that is not the way to freedom: it is the way to slavery.

The failure to believe this truth lay back of the primal sin of the race. "If we eat of this fruit," said the mother of mankind, "we shall surely die." "You shall not surely die," came the prompt reply of the father of lies. "You shall be as gods, knowing good and evil. Instead of finding death, you will find a larger life. Instead of finding slavery, you will find freedom." In other words, the way to be free is to flout the law. Eve was foolish enough to believe this lie, and an innumerable company that no man can number have believed and do believe it still. But nothing could be more utterly and ruinously false. Real freedom can never come except in conformity to law.

For instance: That engine down at the station is both swift and strong. But it is made for a narrow track. As long as it remains upon that track, it is free. When it undertakes to leave it and to go across the country in disregard of the law of its being, it becomes a wreck. That great ship at sea, guided by a little compass no larger than your two fists, is free. But if it decides to toss its compass overboard, it does not win a fuller freedom. It becomes, first a derelict, then a wreck. There is no freedom except in conformity to law. That is a truth that both women and men need to remember in this lawless age.

2. The modern woman is in danger of losing her reticence, her fine feminine delicacy, her moral sensitiveness. Modesty in our day threatens to become obsolete. Nor did it die of a long, lingering disease. It seems rather to have suffered some sudden stroke and to have perished overnight. Blushes are rather rare touches of color except as we buy them ready-made. To my mind this in itself is a threat. For, mark you, modesty is not a matter of trifling importance. A blush is often the crimson banner that a fine moral

sensitiveness floats above the citadel of the soul to show that it has not yet capitulated to the god of the coarse, the common, and the unclean.

The danger of this loss of delicacy and moral fineness on the part of woman is further increased, not only by the fact that she is free, but that she is free at this particular time. Our day is a rather trying one for the very strongest. It seems to have brought a marked increase of temptation along with an equally marked decrease of restraint. Therefore it is not a matter of wonder that this has told peculiarly upon women, many of whom are a bit intoxicated by their new sense of freedom.

(1) Consider this increase of temptation that belongs to our age.

(a) This new day has brought the auto. The auto is a wonderful invention. But all the uses to which it is put are not good. It has changed much of our social life. Young men and women used to meet in the parlor, safeguarded by the atmosphere of the home. But the auto has given them a meeting place. To-day many of them do their courting in the byways of the streets or out in the open country. The curtains of the car are drawn, and there is too little or no restraint.

(b) It has given employment to many young girls in almost every kind of office. Sometimes these offices have an atmosphere that is clean and wholesome. At other times they have an atmosphere that is vicious and hurtful. There a young girl of charm and beauty is often brought into contact with a man without scruples who is far older and more shrewd than herself. The two are thrown much together. As her employer he sees to that. She is often under pressure of economic necessity and is, therefore, eager to keep her place. In multitudes of instances she succeeds and comes out of the furnace without the slightest smell of fire upon her garments. Now and then, however, she loses the fight. She becomes a gold digger. She finds a way to dress well while she works little and thus ends in moral bankruptcy.

(c) To-day we are being flooded by a very deluge of coarse and salacious literature. Some of this is so foul that those who sell it must bootleg it as the dealer in liquor does his wares. The magazine that is said to be most popular among college men and women is one that is digging openly and persistently at those essential and fundamental verities by which our civilization is being held together. Such publications of condensed filth cannot but make for the destruction of faith and the weakening of moral fiber.

(d) Then this is the day of the moving picture. Of course, I am not against all moving pictures. There are many of them that are fine and wholesome. The moving picture show has educational possibilities that are almost unlimited. But unfortunately the industry gets too often into the hands of men whose god is gold. Therefore, in order to attract, they display much that is salacious and sinister in its implications. Young unmarried couples often witness together bedroom scenes that are disgraceful and revolting. They look upon kissing that cannot properly be called kissing at all. It is rather a vulgar chewing of each other's faces. And, what is sadder still, many of our children are regaled by such pictures from their very infancy.

(e) This is the day of the dance in its most vicious form. I am not saying that there might not be a type of dancing that would be innocent and wholesome. But where can you find a sane defender of the modern dance? In my opinion it simply cannot be defended.

It is bad and altogether bad. In this per-
formance couples no longer merely hold hands
as in the old-fashioned way. They are not
even side by side as in the waltz. They are
face to face, and, as a rule, in a close embrace.
The girl is usually very scantily dressed. In
spite of this, there are many that go through
the experience and come out lily white. Of
this I am sure. But, having acknowledged
this, I am convinced that it is a trying ordeal.
There is no doubt, on my part, that the practice of the modern dance tends to destroy
one's moral sensitiveness almost as inevitably
as the handling of the tools of his trade tends
to callous the palms of the blacksmith.

In short, many of our amusements to-day
are not wholesome. They do not rest us and
fit us the better to do our work. They do not
minister to us either physically, mentally,
or spiritually. On the contrary, they tend to
leave us weary and restless, yet with a passion
for more. They are narcotic in their effect
in that they not only produce an appetite for
themselves, but demand a stronger and more
frequent dose. There are literally multitudes
to-day who are amusement fiends. They live
almost wholly in the realm of the senses. They
are thrill hunters. They measure everything

by its capacity to "give a kick" or to "pack a punch." For these conversation is a lost art and to be compelled to spend an evening at home about as welcome as a prison term. It is not to be wondered at, therefore, that this is a day of peculiar temptation, not only to the modern woman, but to the modern man as well.

(2) Hand in hand with this increase of temptation has come a decrease of restraint. Certain barriers against wrongdoing that once were strong have now become weak or have ceased to exist altogether.

(a) First, our day has witnessed a great weakening of the restraint of the home. The family altar has in too many instances either never been builded or has been suffered to fall in ruins. Parental authority has been largely thrown into the discard. There seems to be a new commandment abroad that reads, "Parents, obey your children," for this is customary and the easiest way out of the difficulty. To control children to-day is bad form. To resort to corporal punishment is close akin to witch-burning. Hence many children have their own way from infancy. By the time they are sixteen or seventeen the father and mother are often utterly helpless.

If the girl wishes to keep company with a young man that to the parents seems unfit or if she wishes to engage in amusements that they consider dangerous, they are all but powerless. One of the greatest blessings that could come to America to-day would be a revival of the right kind of parental authority. This would not only make for the safety of our youth, but for their happiness as well. "No child is ever happy whose will is never crossed."

(*b*) There is also a weakening of the restraints of public opinion. Wise men tell us that the youth of our day are more frank and honest than ever before. If they have doubts, they confess the fact with boldness. If there is moral failure, they often confess that with equal boldness. This may be an altogether healthy sign. I am not going to dispute it. But I wonder at times if a part of our frankness about matters that were once more or less taboo in polite conversation is not born of the fact that there is no longer any stern public opinion to scourge us for our frankness. We are losing our capacity to be shocked. The man who has prospered in wrongdoing is not always an object of loathing, but often of envy. Our capacity for righteous indigna-

tion seems all but dead. This lax and effete
public opinion has made it all the easier for
some to so flirt with the questionable as to
lose their moral sensitiveness.

(c) Finally, our day has witnessed a lessen-
ing of those restraints that are born of religion.
The "Thou shalt not" of God has small weight
with vast multitudes. Of course this has always been the case in large measure. But it is
peculiarly true now. We are living in the
midst of a moral and spiritual slump. Most
of us remember well the fine idealism that
was so evident during the closing months of
the World War. But with the signing of the
Armistice a terrible reaction set in. I am not
so pessimistic nor wanting in faith as to believe that this is going to continue. But it
is easy to see that at present the sanctions of
religion are not so compelling as we have
known them. We are suffering from a lost
sense of God. This is evident on every hand.
Naturally this has told upon the modern
woman. One fears at times that she responds
to the appeal of Christ even less readily than
the modern man. Not so long ago it was my
privilege to conduct revival services in a college that was coeducational. Almost every
man responded to the appeal for discipleship.

But the response on the part of the young women represented only about fifty per cent of those in attendance.

3. Then there is the peril of a false ideal.

The ideal of almost every young woman at one time was some other woman, most likely a wife and mother. That is still the ideal with the great majority. But there are those whose ideal seems to be the masculine rather than the feminine. They have somehow come to the conclusion that man all through the centuries has had the better of it. Therefore they want, so far as possible, to do his work and to live his life. In short, they want to be as much like man as possible. This desire leads some to an imitation of men, which imitation is generally disappointing in its results. This is true for the simple reason that the one who imitates another almost invariably imitates that which is worst in the one imitated instead of that which is best. He imitates that which is ridiculous rather than that which is commendable. For instance, think how many good preachers were spoiled by Sam Jones. Of course that was not his fault. They tried to imitate him. But when they undertook this rôle, they imitated those characteristics that were ridiculous rather than those that made him the mighty man he was. The same is true of the imitators of Billy Sunday, and indeed of practically all imitators. Madame Schumann-Heink tells us that she was to sing a rôle for which she had not had opportunity to prepare. But the fact that she had heard a number of other great artists sing it gave her courage. So she sang with their renditions in her mind. What was the result? It was disaster. Her critics said she reproduced every fault of all the artists that she was seeking to imitate. Of course this left little room for the imitation of their excellencies.

But, whether it is imitation or not, women are coming in increasing number to share the vices of men. Swearing among women seems to be on the increase. This is an ugly habit in men. In women it is even more disgusting. Cigarette-smoking among women is certainly on the increase. This habit is decidedly pronounced among certain college and society women. This to my mind is most unfortunate. Of course I am well aware that there are worse habits than cigarette-smoking. I am aware also that women have as much right to smoke as men. But, having confessed this, I maintain that it is coarsening and hurtful.

How tragic, therefore, that so many of those who are to set the standards of society are addicted to this habit! How doubly tragic when you think of such as the future mothers of America! Frankly, I cannot hope nor even imagine that a stronger and finer manhood and womanhood will be nursed in the arms of cigarette-smoking mothers. Dr. Beatrice Hinkle declares that the ideal of virginity among woman is losing its grip. Is she correct? I do not know. We have only one standard to-day. If we are lowering the common level rather than raising it, then there is surely cause for alarm.

4. The modern woman is in danger of shirking her supreme responsibility and missing her supreme opportunity. Too often she fails to marry. At times this is no fault of her own. But at other times it is. Too many of us are the bondslaves of luxury. Here is a woman, for instance, who is making a good salary. She has an opportunity to marry, but she is not willing to face poverty with the man she loves. They wait, and wait, and never marry at all. If she does marry, she is often too quick to break up her home. She knows she is able to make her own way. At other times she shirks the responsibilities and

privileges of motherhood. This is sadly true
of the college-bred woman. Many do not
marry. Those who do have an average of
less than two children. College graduates
do not even replace themselves. The danger
of this is not race suicide. I am not afraid
of that. It is rather that the men and women
of to-morrow will be the sons and daughters
of the underprivileged and handicapped rather
than of those best fitted to give their children
strong bodies and strong minds and the best
opportunity for living an abundant life.

III

How are we to cope with this situation?

1. There must be a strengthening of the
home. There must be a new emphasis placed
on parental authority; and, what is even more
important, a new emphasis on right example.
The home atmosphere must be such as to give
the best possible moral support to character.
In short, it must be vitally and strongly and
winsomely Christian.

2. Men must face up to their responsibilities. There was a time when, if there was
moral delinquency, it was all the fault of
woman. What man had an opportunity to
do, that he had a right to do. But this is

passing. The man who steals, however good his opportunity, is a thief. The man who runs in the face of danger, however safe from being found out, is a coward. The man who goes morally wrong simply because he has opportunity must also face his guilt. It takes two to sin after this fashion. Man must be willing to carry his part of the load.

3. Woman must realize that, while she has much in common with man, she is essentially and eternally different. Too many women seem to be obsessed with the idea that, in order to be equal with men, they must be like them. That is not the case at all. God has given to woman a place that is unique. She is the keeper of the gate of life. The modern woman must be willing to accept this trust with both its crosses and its crowns. That was true of the greatest of women yesterday. It will be true of the greatest to-morrow.

4. Finally, there must be a return to the abiding verities of religion. This is the supreme need. Certainly Christ is the solution of all our problems and the cure for all our ills. The pressing perplexities of our day call for a great spiritual awakening. We must return to God. A new and vital sense of his

presence will result in a better home life,
cleaner amusements, a more bracing and helpful public opinion.   He and he alone can enable us to change our want to wealth and to
make friends even of our foes.

EDUCATION FOR THE NEW DAY

I

WHEN higher education was first opened to women, they adopted without question the curriculum taught in colleges for men. They did not ask whether or not this particular curriculum was the best possible to fit them for their place in the scheme of things. They did not even ask whether or not it was best for the men themselves. Their chief purpose seemed to be to demonstrate that they had intellectual capacities equal to those of men. They were desperately determined to show that they also could master any subject that mere man could master. They felt that it was an absolute necessity that they prove, both to themselves and to the world, the reality of their adequate mental ability.

In this undertaking they have succeeded admirably. We are now ready to confess that women can not only learn French and German, but even Latin and Greek, quite as readily as men. What is more amazing, we must further confess that many of them are quite at home in the realm of mathematics.

Often they move through arithmetic, algebra, geometry, and trigonometry with the air of a conqueror. When we of the stronger sex compare grades with them, we are at times a bit humiliated. Through such comparison we are compelled to acknowledge that, even if woman is the weaker vessel, her weakness is not in the realm of the intellect. Surely she has shown beyond the shadow of a doubt that in mental capacity she is the equal of her brother.

But, while we do not blame women for a desire to demonstrate their capacity to master the masculine curriculum, we are by no means sure that this is a worthy goal. In fact, there are many to-day who seriously question whether or not the average education received by our young men really educates. That is, they do not believe that such education fits in the highest way for the task of living. They believe that the education of to-morrow must be more practical—in other words, that it must have a greater vocational trend. The young man of the future must to a greater and greater degree not only be educated, but educated for something.

With this position I must agree, confessing at the same time a genuine prejudice in favor of a liberal education. Two per cent of our present population are college graduates, and these are filling fifty-nine per cent of our positions of leadership. But we are not to conclude from this that a college course is a sure passport to a position of leadership. There are scores of young men from our best colleges and universities who find themselves right now in a busy world with nothing to sell that the world wants. This is a highly specialized age, and these are not specialists. Therefore they often have either to remain idle or to take positions that give no adequate outlet for their powers.

The tragedy of this situation will not be improved by the mere passing of time. Rather it will grow worse unless our system of education undergoes considerable change. When only few were educated there was great demand for them. Those positions that required trained minds were greater in number than those who were trained. But education is now on the way to becoming universal. It is estimated that ninety per cent of those in school to-day are training more or less definitely to become brain workers. But there is room for only a comparatively small per cent of these in such positions. This means that it is going to be absolutely necessary to train more of our boys back to the farm and back to skilled labor. That is, the education of the future must be not less for the head, but far more for the hand than it is at present.

Now, what I have said of the education of young men applies equally to the education of young women. I am certain that a new and stronger emphasis must be put upon the training of woman for that high vocation which is peculiarly her own. This, however, we shall discuss later. But while the emphasis should be placed there, such training is not enough for the woman of to-day. I feel that every girl should also, as far as possible, be so trained as to enable her to earn her living outside the home if such should become a necessity. This I say for the following reasons:

1. There are those who will never marry. There are a few who will not desire to do so. At least, if they do, such desire will be subordinate and secondary. They are not greatly gifted with the mother instinct. Or they feel that they can make a larger contribution by some career outside the home. Of course those who elect to remain unmarried and to pursue some definite vocation other than that

of wife and mother ought to be trained for that vocation.

Then there are those who will not marry for lack of a fit opportunity. Some of these are among the choicest and best of women. But somehow the right men fail to come. Sometimes this is the result of their working where opportunities for meeting eligible men are rather scant. At other times it comes from the pressure of nearer duties. There is some good cause for delay. By the time this hindrance is removed the harvest is past and the summer ended.

2. Then there are those who will not make a successful marriage. Some will enter into alliances that they will find impossible. Some will have to separate to give their children a decent chance; some to keep their own self-respect; some to save their own souls.

> "Thou art mated to a clown,
> And the grossness of his nature will have weight to drag
> thee down."

Others will fail through their own folly and selfishness. But, whatever be the cause of failure, when separation comes the woman ought to be able to make her own living.

3. There are those who, while happily married, will still find work outside the home

a necessity. Some will have to bear the whole economic burden of the family because of a husband who has lost his health. There are others who will marry men who, while fine in a thousand ways, will yet be incapable of earning sufficient income to provide for the needs of the household. In such cases the wife will find it necessary to work somewhere in order to supplement the inadequate income of her husband. This will often make a position outside the home a necessity.

Then there are wives and mothers who are in large measure relieved of their responsibilities when they are in the neighborhood of fifty. Often by that time the children have gone from the old home. Some have gone into that home from whose bourne no traveler returns. Others have gone to form homes of their own. The wife and husband are now at home very much as they were when he led her, a bride, across the threshold some thirty or more years ago. To such a mother, with her children gone, life tends to lose much of its meaning. Her husband still has his business. The change has not meant so much to him. But to her it has meant a great deal. There are no longer little faces to be washed, no patter of baby feet, no little hands folded for the evening prayer. The one-time busy mother now has sufficient leisure to be lonely. She feels herself superannuated while in middle life. Happy is such a woman, therefore, if she is able to give herself, at least in part, to some form of useful work outside the home. Those who do not have to earn can certainly do work of a religious and social nature.

II

But, while considering it wise that our young women be so trained as to enable them to make their own way in the world, should such a course become necessary, I am also convinced that every one of them should be trained for the highest of all vocations, that of making a home. Every girl ought to be trained for home-building for the following reasons:

1. This is the vocation that the majority of girls are sure to follow. Most girls are going to marry. That is certain. That is what they ought to do. That is what they must do, or we face racial decline and ruin. How foolish, therefore, to fail to give special and definite training for the career that the vast majority of our girls will certainly follow and ought to follow.

2. Not only will the majority of girls be sure to marry, but any one of them may marry. I am aware of the fact that some from childhood decide against marriage. I know there are some who from their tender years pledge their lifelong allegiance to a career. I am further aware of the fact that some of these remain true to their first love to the end of the chapter. But, having confessed all this, I am still convinced that any woman might marry. Frankly, I would not risk a single woman in the world if the right man should come along. Therefore, since the majority are sure to marry, since any might marry, all ought to be trained for this important career.

3. Every girl ought to be trained for home-making because the measure of her all-round readiness for this most worthful task will be the measure of her success in it. "They that were ready went in to the feast." That is not surprising. Those are the ones who always enter, and the door is shut in the face of all others. God does not shut the door, man does not shut it, an evil fate does not shut it. Every door shuts automatically in the face of the one who is not ready to enter.

For instance, while I was in college I read

quite a bit about the opera "Parsifal." I
had never attended grand opera, but I decided to see and hear this. I reached the
theater ahead of time and remained to the
end. There were those present who said that
it was wonderful. I suppose they were correct.
I did not argue the question then and am not
disposed to do so now. But, so far as I was
personally concerned, it was a dreary and
taxing failure. They that were ready went
in to the feast, and the door was shut. I was
among those who were shut out. But this was
not due to some blunder on the part of an
usher. I was not shut out by a tricky and dis-
honest manager. I was shut out by my own
unreadiness.

This principle holds true in every department of life. What a feast is in the literature
of the world! But in how many faces the door
remains shut because they are not ready!
I stood in the Louvre and watched the crowds
pace by. What a wealth of art was there!
There one could see some of the greatest
dreams that genius had ever spilled upon the
canvas. But many never saw them. They
did not enter the feast because they were not
ready. They remained without, bored to
extinction.

Why do so many marriages fail? Why do
so many enter into this beautiful and holy
relationship expecting to find heaven and end
by finding hell? There are many answers to
this question. But one big and inclusive
answer is this: Those who marry are so often
not ready. This is true in the case of both
men and women. It is possibly more true of
the woman of to-day than of yesterday. In
1926 there was one State that had more
divorces than marriages. Only a minority
entered the feast. In the face of the majority
the door was shut. They were not ready.
To save our girls from this tragedy every one
of them should be trained for wifehood and
home-making.

III

But what is to be the nature of this preparation? A full answer to this question is at once
beyond my purpose and ability. However,
I am going to venture a few suggestions that
I am convinced are fundamental.

1. First, every girl should be trained to
appreciate the supreme worth and importance
of the home. No nation can possibly attain
to real greatness without a great home life.
It has been well said that our own nation

owes its greatness to the fact that it has been a nation of home-builders more than to any other one cause. The same might be said of certain other nations, especially of England. The home is the maker and builder of the nation. No people will ever rise higher than the homes that give them birth, and none will ever sink below that level. The home will either be the salvation of our civilization, or it will be its destruction.

Not only ought every girl be brought to realize the importance of the home, but she ought also to be trained to a new appreciation of woman's strategic position in the home. It is safe to say that back of every great home there is a great wife and mother. It is safe to say also that she who is great as wife and mother is truly great as a servant of humanity. There are many who seem to forget this. There are some even foolish enough to regard the home-building as mere drudgery. Children in the opinion of these are little more than so many stones in the prison that shuts them away from the big outside world of achievement There is a contempt for the home in certain quarters that is full of danger both to those possessed of such contempt and to the home as well.

These false and harmful views must be corrected. We rejoice in the fact that the woman who works outside the home is often making a worth-while and highly important contribution. Not infrequently she is doing her work at a definite call from God. Honor to her who toils at any worthful task. But honor above all to her who gives herself to the supreme task, that of building a home It was not intended that every woman should occupy this high position. But, in my opinion, the woman who deliberately turns from it abdicates her supremest throne and stops her ears to the deepest and sweetest secret of human blessedness.

2. Every girl should be trained for the making of a home. The art of rightly organizing and managing a home is of vast importance. Like all truly worth-while tasks, it is difficult and exacting. It costs something to be a really successful wife and mother. Such a task needs both culture and consecration. I doubt if there is a railroad president or a manager of a large business corporation to-day who puts more of thought and of genius into his work than Mrs. Susanna Wesley put into the ordering of her home. I am absolutely sure, too, that none of them will accomplish

anything that approximates her marvelous results.

(1) To help toward this goal she should be taught domestic science. The man who achieves the best in any business or profession expects to be thoroughly trained for his work. But too often our girls enter upon the big business of home-making without any training whatever. In 1926 there were approximately fifteen hundred thousand young women in the United States who entered into the marriage relationship. It is estimated that fifty per cent of these knew nothing about keeping a home. They did not know how to buy, clean house, cook, sew, or even wash dishes. It is not to be wondered at that so many such marriages end in failure. I know that "man shall not live by bread alone." It is equally true that neither man nor woman can live without it. To try to build a house of happiness upon ignorance and slovenliness, and upon food served out of paper bags upon paper plates, is to trust a foundation more shifting than sand. A well-ordered home is a blessing from the Lord. What we eat and how it is prepared has more to do with our success or failure in the marriage relation as well as in all else than we often believe.

(2) She should be trained for motherhood. To this end, (*a*) She should be taught adequately to appreciate the meaning of personality and the dignity and worth of the individual life. What the mother sees in her child will in a large measure determine her estimate of the significance of her task. (*b*) So far as possible she ought to know childhood and how to deal with it physically, intellectually, and spiritually. (*c*) Finally, she should be made to realize that the greatest contribution a mother can make to her child is herself. No blessing can possibly come to a home that is quite so great as a genuinely consecrated, cultured, clear-visioned, sympathetic mother. Blessed indeed is the bride whose previous training fits her for such a vocation, and blessed, also, the child of such a mother.

3. Finally, every girl, and every boy as well, should be taught a proper conception of marriage. This institution lies at the foundation of all else. It is the basis upon which rests the home. If the marriage relationship comes to be a thing of rubbish and sand, then the home will topple into ruins. With the wreck of the home will inevitably come the wreck

of all else that is of vital worth in our civilization.

Now, in seeking a proper conception of marriage, I know of no authority equal to Jesus Christ. This I say, realizing that there are many to-day who feel that his teaching on this question is antiquated and that they themselves can formulate a far better and more workable plan. But, in spite of all those who in this matter flout the authority of Jesus both by precept and practice, my conviction remains that the Christian conception of marriage is the only right conception. It is right in that it fits into human need. It is right in that it is conducive at once to the highest happiness and highest usefulness both to those immediately concerned and to society as a whole.

What that conception is in its fullness it is not my purpose to discuss here. I mention only a few fundamental facts.

(1) Marriage is a divine institution. It is a part of God's purpose for the race. Those really married are bound by something far greater than a civil contract. They are reckoned as joined by God himself. "What, therefore, God hath joined together let not man put asunder."

(2) Marriage is the supreme human relationship. It is to take precedence over all others. The obligation of child to parent is very holy and very binding. But even this must yield in importance to the relationship of marriage. "For this cause shall a man leave father and mother and shall cleave to his wife. And they twain shall be one flesh."

(3) Marriage is for life. It is for "better or for worse, for richer or poorer, till death do us part." It is not to last for just a year or for a dozen years. It is not to last till the first quarrel. It is to last till the sunset. Except for unfaithfulness, there is no divorce with the privilege of remarriage.

Now, it is not claimed that those entering marriage with this conception always make a success of the enterprise. But this much may be claimed with boldness and conviction; those so entering stand the best possible chance of making a success. The Christian conception of marriage is certainly the best that has yet been tried. To be convinced of this, it is only necessary to look on the practical tests that are being made all about us. There are those who are marrying and divorcing and marrying again without the slightest regard to the laws of God. What is the outcome? Do such convince you that they have arrived? Have they found real happiness? Have they given their children a fair chance? In what respect have they lived more richly and usefully than those who have clung to the conviction that marriage is a sacred and binding something? In no respect at all. They have only cheated themselves in a way too tragic for tears.

Companionate marriage has recently been suggested as a panacea for our marital ills. But there is not the slightest hope in this direction. In my opinion such marriage is a breach of good morals. Certainly it is contrary to the plan of Christ. But, aside from all this, it is utterly condemned at the bar of common sense. To enter a companionate marriage is to court failure and to give a pressing invitation to disaster. To succeed in marriage, those so doing must enter to succeed. They must foreclose their minds against the possibility of failure. In this respect the adventure of marriage is not peculiar. It is like every other enterprise.

For instance, the girl who decides to get an education, but determines at the same time that she will quit school as soon as she meets a difficulty, is not likely to startle the world by her scholarship. The one who begins the study of music with her mind made up to leave off as soon as the new wears away will never learn music. The same is equally true of those entering law, or teaching, or any other profession. If you cannot face the difficult; if you cannot stand up to the job when its poetry has, for the time, become dull prose; if you cannot keep on when radiant romance has changed, for the moment, to drab drudgery —then you will not likely win in any worthy undertaking. Certainly you are not likely to win in the big, taxing task of marriage. Here surely you must be willing to face your problems patiently, courageously, and loving-ly and with high determination to succeed. It is possible for those entering marriage with the best of intentions to fail. But those who marry with their minds made up to balk at the first hard place are almost sure to fail. Therefore, it is of highest importance that we safeguard our youth by teaching them a proper conception of marriage.

So to train our girls, therefore, as to enable them to make a living outside the home, is often wise and necessary. Some of them will be compelled to do this kind of work. To train them for the task of wifehood and home-making is more important still. There the majority will surely invest themselves. That is what they ought to do. There is where they will live most normally and most abundantly. There is where they will give with greatest abandon, and in so doing they will be privileged to receive.

CHRIST AND WOMAN

THE attitude of Jesus toward woman was altogether unique. Every other founder of a religion seems to have accepted with the men of his day the conviction that woman is inferior. Every other gave instructions that were peculiarly for women. But Jesus is grandly different. He never uttered one single word that indicated that he considered woman in any sense inferior to man. He never said anything to her that he might not have said with equal propriety to man. Nor did he ever say anything to man that he might not just as fittingly have said to woman. In fact, as another has pointed out, if we had only the Gospels to go by, it would never occur to us that woman at any time or anywhere was regarded as an inferior. Certainly Christ looked upon her, not merely as a woman, but as a human being of equal worth and standing as man.

To be convinced of the truth of this it is only necessary to consider the following facts:

1. Christ recognizes that men and women are alike in their moral and spiritual natures.

(1) They are the same in their hungers and

18284

thirsts. Throughout the Bible man is represented as being possessed of spiritual hungers
and spiritual thirsts that only God can satisfy.
"As the hart panteth after the water brook,
so panteth my soul after thee, O God." That
is a thirst that belongs to every man. But it
belongs no less to every woman. It is not a
sex characteristic. It is a characteristic of the
race. Christ recognized that thirst as belong-
ing even to a woman who was an outcast.
Hence he said to her with abounding confidence, "If thou knewest the gift of God, and
who it is that saith to thee, Give me to drink;
thou wouldest have asked of him, and he
would have given thee living water."

(2) Jesus recognized man and woman as
bound by the same moral law. There were
not certain virtues that were necessary for
woman, but of which man had no need. How
strikingly is this fact brought out in that
sordid story of the woman caught in her
shame! There they come, a group of self-
righteous Pharisees. They are dragging in
their soiled hands this bit of tarnished womanhood. They fling her down before the Master
with these words: "She is a sinner. We are
eyewitnesses of her guilt. Moses says she
should be stoned. What do you say?"

"Stone her if you will," he replied, "provided you yourselves are clean. But let no man dare fling a stone who is guilty of the same sin. What is wrong for her is wrong for you."

That was revolutionary teaching. Nothing like it had ever before been heard. Of course, decency in women was expected and required. But not so with men. Here, however, is One who tells us that God looks with the same eye on sin, whether it be the sin of a man or the sin of a woman. We have not fully come to agree with Christ yet. Some are still ready to excuse in men what is inexcusable in women. But just so long as we keep that attitude we are going to make it easier for both men and women to go wrong. Remember, whatever are *our* standards, Jesus has only one. We must all stand before the judgment seat of Christ, whether we be men or women. We are all bound by the same moral law.

(3) Christ admits all into his fellowship by the same door. If a man goes wrong, wanders into the far country and wastes his substance with riotous living, if he will repent, Christ will give him welcome back to his heart. But no less free is his offer of mercy and of pardon to woman. It is hard for us to

give the woman a second chance. But it is not so for Jesus. To this soiled and bedraggled woman, who had been cast in her shame at his feet, he said, "Go thy way and sin no more." We are all admitted, therefore, by the same door into the friendship of Jesus Christ our Lord.

(4) Our Lord made as profound spiritual disclosures to women as he did to men.

That was a great hour when Peter talked with the Master at Cæsarea Philippi. "Who do you say that I am?" asked Jesus. Peter, illuminated by the Holy Spirit, answered, "Thou art the Christ, the Son of the living God." But Peter and his fellow apostles were not the only ones to whom Christ made this great disclosure of himself. Before he made it to these he made it to this woman at the well. "I know that Messiah cometh," she says wistfully. "When he is come, he will tell us all things." "I that speak unto thee am he," answered Jesus. It was to this woman also that Christ revealed this deep truth concerning the nature of God, "God is a Spirit: and they that worship him must worship him in spirit and in truth."

It was to a woman that he gave one of his most satisfying disclosures of the after life.

Martha has lost her brother. She is face to
face with that age-old heartache that comes
through death and separation. "Thy brother
shall rise again," Jesus tells her. But the
resurrection seems to Martha to be so far
away. Death, with its bitter grief, is so near
and real. Therefore Martha replies, with
some impatience I imagine, "I know that he
shall rise again in the resurrection at the last
day." "But," she seems to imply, "that is
so far away." Then Jesus replies, "I am the
resurrection and the Life." I am not in the
distance. I am present. I am in the here and
now. That is, the dead are not dead in reality.
They have not even lain down to sleep until
some far-off resurrection. On the contrary,
they are alive forevermore.

Then it was to a woman that Jesus first
showed himself after he had risen from the
dead. This he did not for any arbitrary reason. He did it because she of all others was
best fitted to receive the vision. Mary was
earliest at the tomb. She came with a love
that simply could not let him go. Therefore,
to her Christ first showed himself alive. It
was she also to whom he first gave the high and
glad commission to go tell others that he had
risen from the dead.

2. Jesus enlisted women in his service just as gladly as he enlisted men.

(1) It was through a holy woman that he gained admission in our humanity. He could not accomplish his incarnation without the aid of consecrated womanhood. He accepted the ministry of women by sharing their hospitality. There were possibly a number of homes that were open to Jesus. The story of one of these has become a classic. We are so well acquainted with the home over which Martha presided that we almost feel that we have visited there. I fancy that there was no spot that Jesus loved more in the days of his mature manhood than this Bethany home. Sometimes Martha was a bit fussy. Sometimes she worried too much over what she was going to have for dinner. But Jesus was always delighted to be in her home. And it stands written in the record that he loved Martha and her sister and Lazarus. You notice the man is mentioned last.

(2) Jesus accepted the testimony of women. When as a baby he was brought into the temple there were two people that had sufficient spiritual insight to discern the Christ that was hidden away in the little child. One of them was Simeon. You remember how he took the

child in his arms and prayed that beautiful prayer, "Lord, now lettest thou thy servant depart in peace: for mine eyes have seen thy salvation." But his testimony was no more clear and no more confident than that of the prophetess Anna. She spoke to the people boldly of this child, telling them that he was the one hope of all who were living in expectation of the dawning of a new day.

Christ even accepted the testimony of that outcast woman with whom he spoke at the well. When she had found who the man was to whom she was speaking, she left her water vessel and hurried back into the city. She went with this message: "Come and see the man who told me all things that ever I did. Is not this the Christ?" And Jesus accepted her testimony. Not only did Jesus accept it, but the people accepted it also. It stands written in the record that "many believed because of the saying of the woman." And since that day an innumerable company that no man can number have also believed because of the sayings of consecrated women.

3. Jesus was quite as liberal in his praise of women as he was in his praise of men. In fact, I think, if you will look over the most commendatory things he said, you will find

that the majority of them were spoken either to or concerning women. Who was the giver in the Gospels that beyond all others met the approval of Christ? It was not one of the twelve. It was a woman. It was that poor widow that cast two mites into the treasury, which was all her living. Who was the most approved worker? Here again we must answer that it is not a man, but a woman. About a certain woman named Mary he said, "She hath done what she could." That is, she hath done her best. No greater word of praise can be uttered about any human soul than that. Christ delights to be trusted. We all do. Who is the one that more than all others rejoices the heart of Christ by believing in him? Here again I think we must give the palm to a woman. The faith of that Roman soldier was wonderful. So marvelous it was that it even took Jesus by surprise. He said, "I have not found so great faith, no, not in Israel." But he found it outside. He found it in the heart of a heathen woman, this woman come to him on behalf of her afflicted daughter. When she made her appeal she at first met with silence, then with seeming refusal. But she persisted. At last Jesus turned with face alight with joy and said, "O woman, great is thy faith: be it unto thee even as thou wilt."

Of all the offerings that we can make to our Lord, there is none so great as our love. "If I bestow all my goods to feed the poor, and if I give my body to be burned, and have not love, it profiteth me nothing. . . . Now abideth faith, hope, love, these three; but the greatest of these is love." Who is the outstanding lover of the New Testament? John calls himself the disciple whom Jesus loved. He himself was also a great and ardent lover. But Jesus seems to give first place to a woman. This is the scene. It is night. Jesus is dining in the house of a Pharisee named Simon. A woman comes in from out of the dark. She takes the cascade of her hair and wipes the feet of her Lord that are already wet with her tears. Simon is horrified that the Master should allow himself to be touched by such a woman. But Jesus says of her, "Her sins, which are many, are forgiven her; for she loved much."

Thus it is evident that Jesus regarded men and women as equals. Therefore I feel safe in saying that this larger freedom that women now enjoy has come through principles enunciated and set in motion by him. It is Jesus that has knocked the shackles off the hands of womanhood. I have not forgotten that I said that economic conditions are responsible for many of the changes that have taken place in the status of woman. But Christ is back of all, moving on to the accomplishment of his purpose. Every step that woman has taken from the bondage of yesterday to the freedom of to-day she owes to Jesus Christ our Lord.

II

What is the basis of this equality on the part of men and women that seems so clearly taught by our Lord? It is not physical strength. Men and women are not equal physically. In a fistic encounter the average woman would have little chance against the average man. In a world largely dominated by physical force the woman would of necessity be a subordinate. It is in such a world that she has lived through long centuries. This fact, above all else, accounts for her being looked upon by all nations as an inferior. What, then, is the basis of equality between man and woman as taught by Jesus? It is, as another has indicated, the recognition of the supremacy of the spiritual; for, while men and women are not equal physically, they are equal spiritually.

Not only does a recognition of the supremacy of the spiritual lead naturally to the emancipation of woman, but it serves as a cure for countless other ills.   Faith in force has ever been the mother of tragedy.   This is true for the simple reason that whoever believes in the supremacy of force will resort to force whenever the necessity for so doing seems to arise.   Such necessity has seemingly arisen with frightful frequency throughout all human history.   It was faith in the god of force that was responsible for the World War.   It is this same faith that has resulted in countless conflicts that have done little more than lower moral standards, blight ideals, wreck homes, and overspread our continents with graves. It is safe to say that nothing has been more costly to our world than the worship of physical force.

It is not surprising, therefore, that Jesus fixed his faith upon the spiritual.   In the very beginning of his ministry he made a definite choice between the way of the great military chieftains of the earth and the way of the spirit.   "All these things," said the tempter, showing him the kingdoms of the world and the glory of them, "will I give thee, if thou wilt fall down and worship me." To which he replied, "Get thee hence, Satan: for it is written, Thou shalt worship the Lord thy God, and him only shalt thou serve." To that decision and choice he remained steadfastly true to the end. Never did he resort to physical force as a means of bringing in his kingdom. When he preached, it was upon the Spirit that he depended. "The Spirit of the Lord is upon me, because he hath anointed me to preach." It was in reliance upon spiritual power that he performed his cures and worked his wonders. When at last he was arrested he refused to deliver himself by physical means, though he declared that he had it in his power to summon twelve legions of angels for the task. He allowed force to drag him away and nail him to a cross. Then, when force had done its worst, he took its very victory and through the might of the spiritual began then and there the conquest of the world.

III

What should be the outcome of this new freedom that has come to woman at the hands of Christ?

It ought to awaken a genuine gratitude. It ought to beget a profound sense of obligation. It ought to lead every one of you to say with strong conviction, "I am a debtor." In fact, if such is not the result, your freedom has done little for you. To be wanting in a sense of obligation is to remain a moral dwarf, a spiritual infant. A baby is a lovely something, but he is shameless in his utter lack of any sense of gratitude or obligation. If he is in pain, you may walk him for hours. But when you put him down he will not thank you. He will not say, "After an effort like that I am under obligations to be quiet." He will only utter a wild wail. The only possible excuse for such conduct is to remember that he is a baby. But as we grow to maturity, we should put away childish things.

"I am a debtor." That is a word that befits the lips of every one of us, whether man or woman. It is demanded of every creature, even of every thing, that it give an account of itself in terms of service. The creature that will not serve we call a parasite. If it belongs to the lower order of creation, we make war against it and do our best to exterminate it. If it belongs to the highest order, we have to seek to convert it. Failing in this, we must

tolerate it and leave it to its own wretchedness. If it chances to be a piece of machinery
that refuses to serve, we junk it. There is
no place for the useless. Every flower that
blooms must bloom for another. Every bird
that sings must sing for another. God himself must bend his broad shoulders under the
burdens and needs of a universe. And all who
are made in his image are under obligations
to be workers together with him.

"Let my people go, that they may serve
me." That was God's command with regard
to his chosen people in the long ago. That is
his purpose in this larger freedom that has
come to woman. To every girl I would say,
You have not been set free simply for yourself.
You have not come to this day of opportunity
that you may have your fling and do as you
please. You have not entered into your land
of promise that you may toss responsibility
to the four winds and live your own life. No
other woman was ever so weighted with obligations as the woman of to-day. None other
was ever so deeply in debt. This is true for
the simple reason that none other ever had
so great a chance. Great obligations always
go arm in arm with great opportunities.

Now, in order that you may discharge your

debt in an adequate fashion, you must seek to be the best that God made it possible for you to be. "Thou art Peter," said Jesus to a blundering fisherman one day, "but thou shalt be a rock of Christ-like character." Peter heard him and took the trail toward his best possible self. He made many a mistake. Once he became an utter coward. But he always had the courage to begin again. He kept setting his face toward the heights, and the world is the richer to this day because he lived. There is an upward trail that leads from where you sit. If you take it and persist, it will bring you to your largest possible self.

(1) You owe it to the world to become your best physically. Our day has brought to woman the right to play. Athletic sports are now open to you, and you can enjoy them without being classed as a tomboy. What is even more important, you can profit by them without shame. It used to be close akin to a disgrace for a woman to be robust. Good health, if an asset at all, was a rather questionable one. A woman's main business was to be a fragile creature with the slenderest waist possible. To this end she must struggle, even if she impaired her usefulness and took

a few years off her life in the effort. To-day woman has a free hand at the fine business of good health. Therefore she ought in so far as possible to make a success of it.

(2) It is needless to tell you that you ought to look well to your intellectual furnishings. This is a positive duty to those who have given you your opportunity, to society, and to your Lord. Every worth-while thing you know will make you a better servant of mankind. Know as much as you can. Better still, learn to use what you know. Burke was right when he said, "Reading and much reading is good, but the power of classifying and using the matter read is better." Happy is she whose training enables her to marshal all her resources for the putting over of a definite task.

(3) Finally, you are under the weightiest of obligations to be your best spiritually. It is only trite to say that there is no necessary connection between high intellectuality and high morality. You may know much and be very little. You may know much and do little. To do your best you must be your best. To be your best you must "let this mind be in you that was also in Christ Jesus." You must present your bodies to him as a living sacrifice. To seek to keep your life is certain-

ly to lose it. To give it away is surely to keep it unto life eternal.

When King Arthur lay dying, you remember how he gave his sword to his last remaining knight and ordered him to fling it back into the lake in good faith. But before throwing it away he decided to have one more look at it. So he drew it from the scabbard and watched it sparkle and gleam in the moonlight. The beauty of it fascinated him; so he hid it among the bushes and went and told the king a fictitious story.

The king knew that he was speaking falsely; so he sent him again. But a second time the lure of its beauty held him. A second time he hid it among the rushes and went and told the king a fictitious story. This time the king was angry. He raised himself upon his elbow and, pointing toward the lake, said, "Go and do my bidding, or I will rise from my death-bed to slay you." The knight hurried away, and, without trusting himself to look at the sword, flung it far into the lake. But before the sword touched the water a wonderful hand seized it, wielded it three times, and then vanished. And the knight knew that he had not flung the sword away to rust at the bottom of the lake. He had only passed it to a hand

mightier than his own. So my last word to
you is this: Fling yourself away in Christ.
He will not let you lose your life. He will enable you in the fullest sense to save it.

DATE DUE

DEC 3 '63	MAY 11 '73	APR 22 '81	
-R 11 '64	MAY 29 '73	APR 13 '83	
MAY 19 64	OCT 15 '73		
MAY 23 '64	MAY 4 '74		
SEP 18 '64	NOV 14 '74		
ESC 7 '64	Dec. 9. '74		
JAN 5 '65	JAN 14 '75		
	JAN 28 '75		
FEB 18 '66	MAR 21 '75		
MAY 19 66	APR 12 '76		
MAY 26 67	DEC 6 '76		
MAR 1 '89	FEB 22 '77		
MAR 19 69			
JAN 8 '71			
JAN 21 '72			
M			
APR 11 '73			
APR 28 '73			